The Fabled Land

by
Stephanie Miller

Windyfoot Publishing • Los Angeles, California

Published in the United States by Windyfoot Publishing
1146 North Central Avenue 312 Glendale, CA 91202
coloringadventures@gmail.com

10 9 8 7 6 5 4 3 2 1
Printed in the United States of America

LIBRARY OF CONGRESS CATALOGING-IN-PUBLISHING DATA Miller, Stephanie
The Fabled Land

ISBN 0692555269
First Edition

Cover design by Sanae Robinson and Stephanie Miller

To purchase a copy of this book, please visit ColoringAdventures.com

For all my beloved teachers

About The Fabled Land

Welcome to Coloring Adventures! This book is designed to help you relax, meditate and celebrate your creativity. Inspired by Indian Moghul histories, Persian miniatures, Moorish architecture, North African textiles and tiles and other ancient art, the symbols, stories and images are fanciful and dreamlike, and many are quite personal. All of the illustrations are created by hand without the use of rulers or other aids. You will find imperfections which help make this coloring book part of a vibrant, living art project that we are creating together. Step onto the path, trust your inner compass and enjoy this journey through beautiful, exotic lands.

My life has been profoundly influenced by the transformative power of meditation. I hope this book will provide you with a way to relax and contemplate while you color. You'll notice a short phrase on the facing page opposite each illustration. These are prompts inviting you to explore new ideas deeply while you color. Some are affirmations I have found meaningful in my own life and work. All of these contemplations are intended to connect with the basic goodness and dignity that we all share.

When you complete a page, please take a picture and share it with us at facebook/coloringadventures. And if you can take a moment, please write a review of this book at Amazon.com to let your fellow coloring fans know what you think. Your heartfelt good word is the best way to spread the joy of contemplative coloring.

Enjoy your unique coloring experience. May it be beautifully yours.

About Stephanie Miller

Stephanie Miller is a happy refugee from corporate America with a degree in design, and now working full-time as an artist and published author of the poetry collection Derby Poems and The Wisdom of the Kitchen Manifesto. Trained as a meditation instructor, she is also a Zen archery student and loves horses. She is a native Southern Californian who is always up for a trip anywhere in the world, and anywhere her imagination leads her.

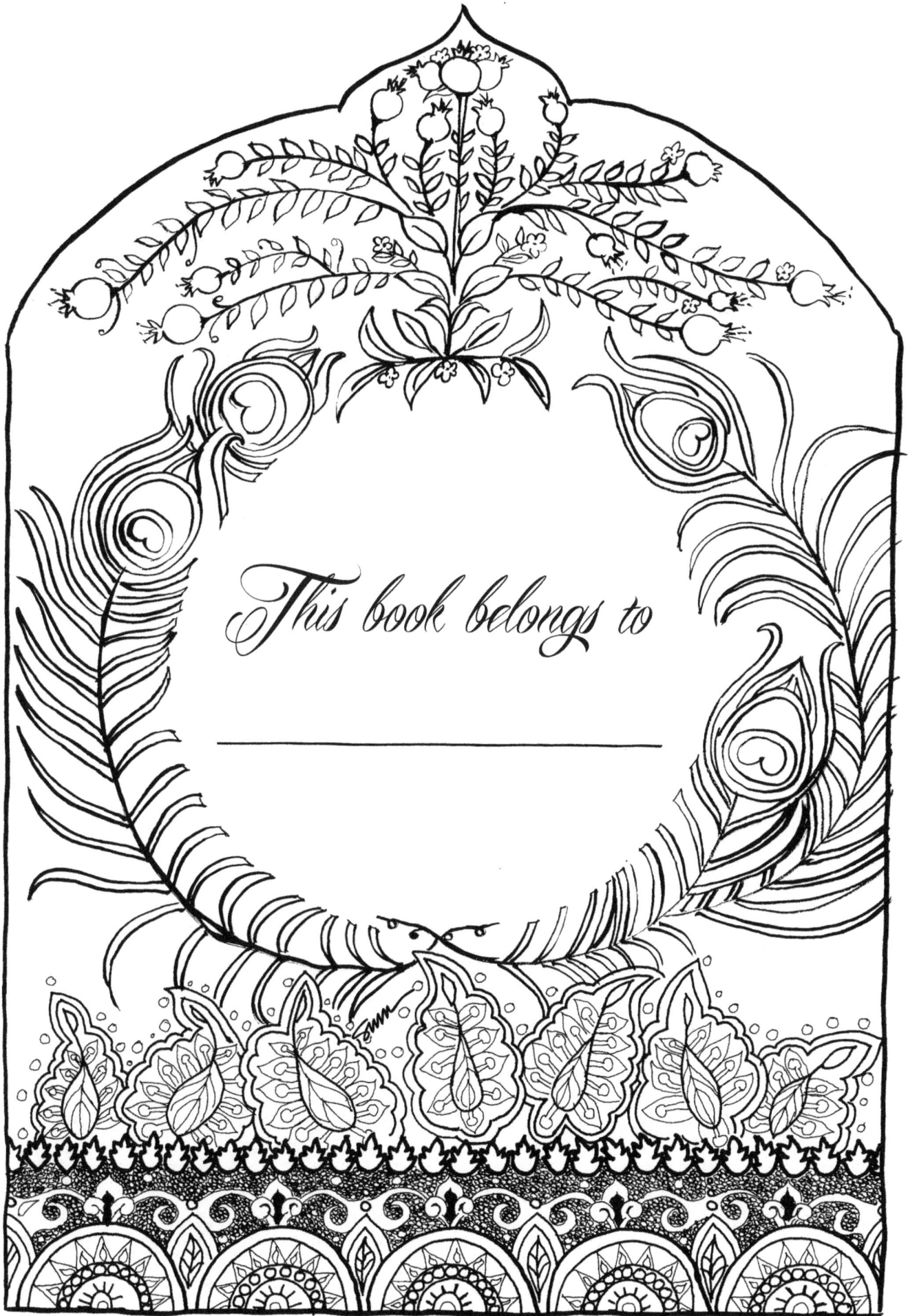

This book belongs to

_____

Inspire kindness

There is enough of everything you need

Be open to receiving more

Be grateful

Appreciate differences

Respect order

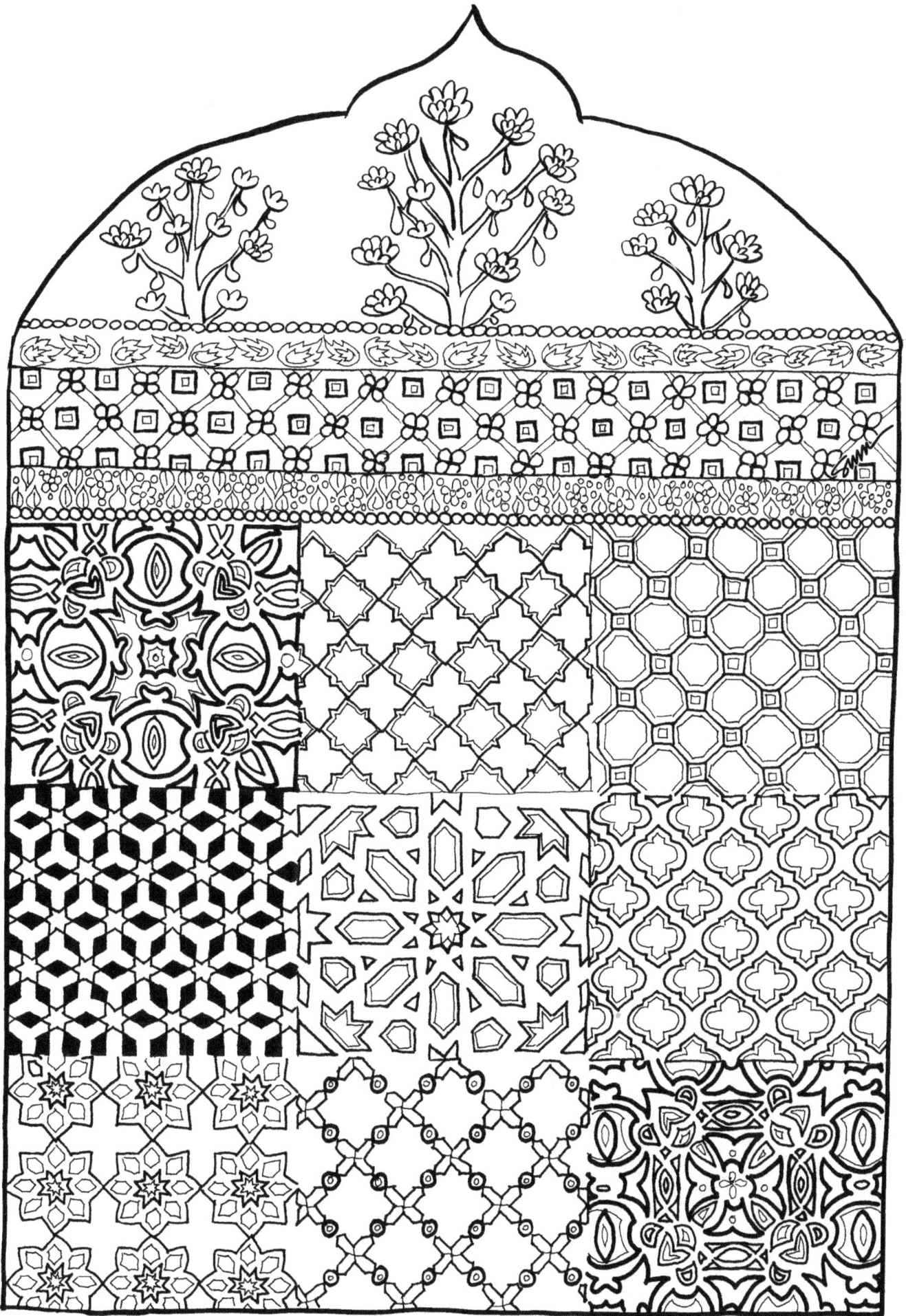

You are at home in the world

Appreciate your own worthiness

Be gentle

Follow your intuition

Trust your experience

Listen

Cultivate joy

Embrace change

©2015

Liberate yourself

You can create the time you need

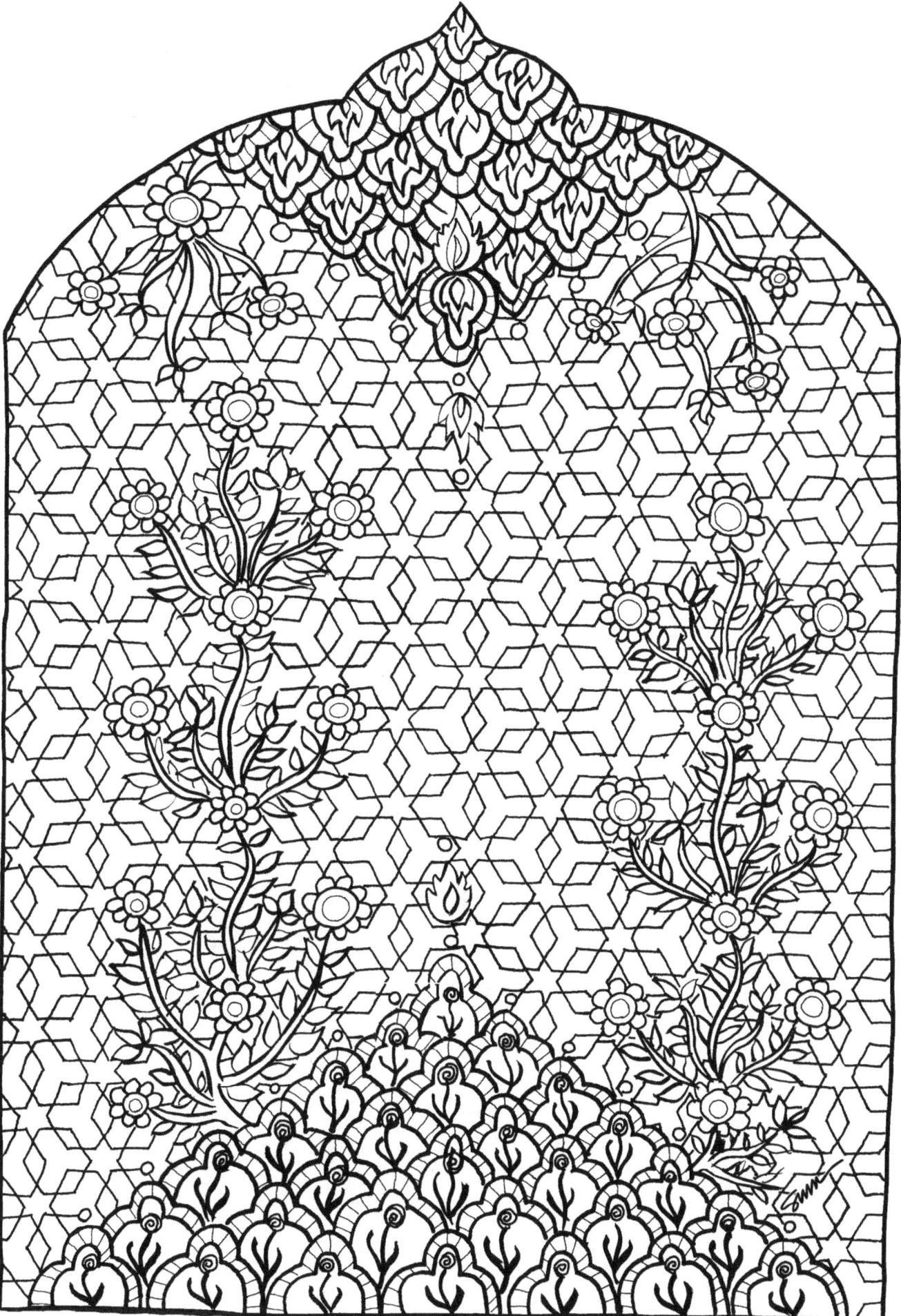

Shine

Nurture silence

Be creative

Know that you are basically good

Follow the love

Invoke magic

Give with an open hand

Pause

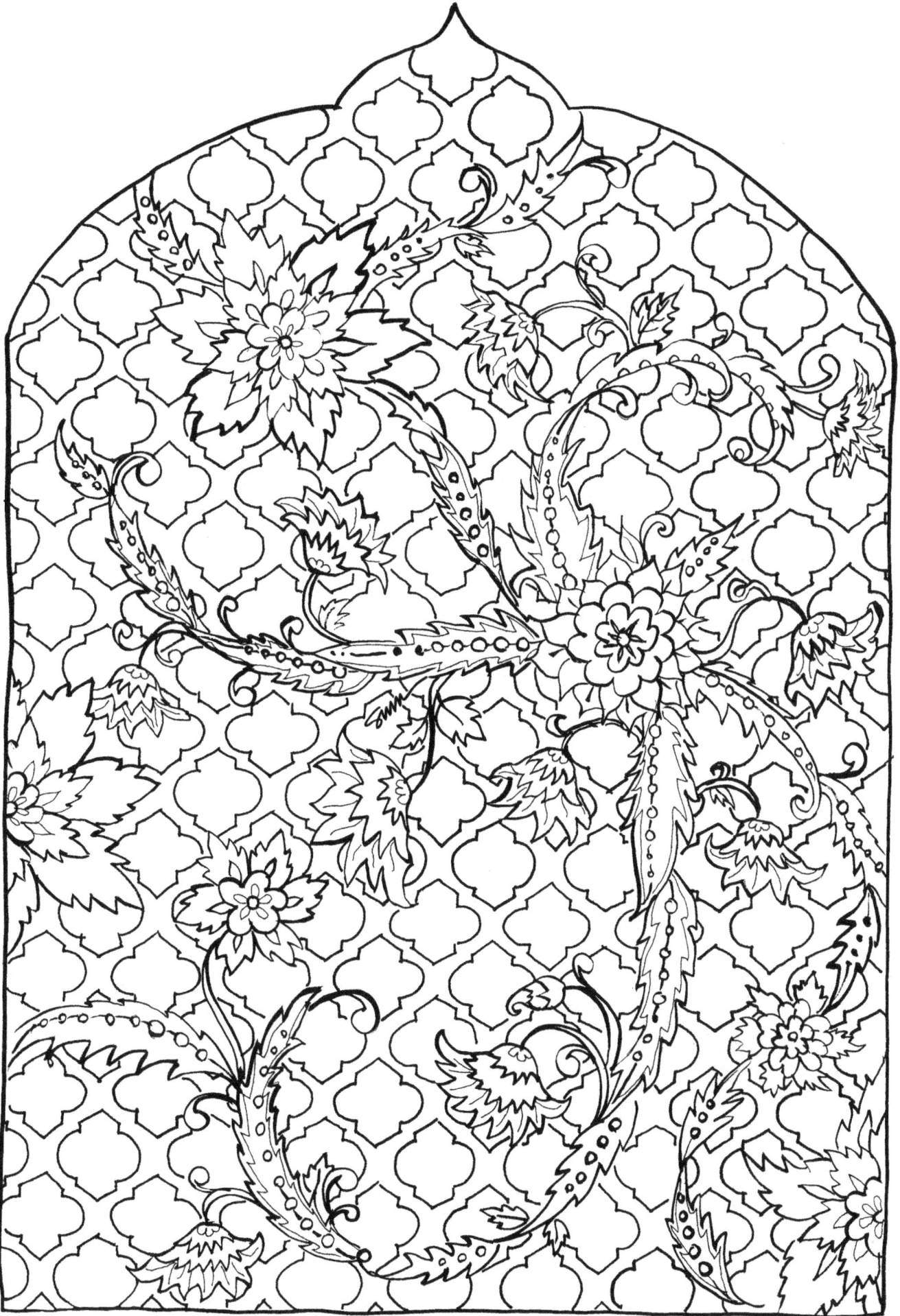

Acknowledge beauty

Just be

Resist self-hatred

Lead with your vulnerability

Believe in possibility

Face what you fear

Bloom in unexpected places

Be brave

Magnetize abundance

Transmute life's poisons

Mix things up

Contemplate peace

Contemplative Coloring

Close your eyes and bring your attention to your breathing. Rest in the present moment. Open your eyes and select an image that inspires you. Read the short phrase on the facing page. Think about the meaning of the words together and about each individual word. Begin coloring. Periodically notice your breathing, return to the phrase, think about its meaning again. Each phrase is listed below.

1. Inspire kindness
2. There is enough of everything you need
3. Be open to receiving more
4. Be grateful
5 Appreciate differences
6. Respect order
7. You are at home in the world
8. Appreciate your own worthiness
9. Be gentle
10. Follow your intuition
11. Trust your experience
12. Listen
13. Cultivate joy
14. Embrace change
15. Liberate yourself
16. You can create the time you need
17. Shine
18. Nurture silence

19. Be creative
20. Know that you are basically good
21. Follow the love
22. Invoke magic
23. Give with an open hand
24. Pause
25. Acknowledge beauty
26. Just be
27. Resist self-hatred
28. Lead with your vulnerability
29. Believe in possibility
30. Face what you fear
31. Bloom in unexpected places
32. Be brave
33. Magnetize abundance
34. Transmute life's poisons
35. Mix things up
36. Contemplate peace

Find the Fauna and Flora

In addition to the countless flowers, stars and patterns, see if you can find everything on the list below.

☐ Blue Heron

☐☐☐ Bunches of grapes

☐ Cow

☐☐☐☐ Crows

☐ Dove

☐ Dragon

☐☐ Elk

☐ Falcon

☐☐☐ Hummingbirds

☐☐☐ Jaguars

☐☐☐ Loons

☐☐☐ Moons

☐ Owl

☐ Panther

☐☐ Parrots

☐☐☐ Rabbits

☐ Rooster

☐ Scorpion

☐ Stork

☐ Weasel

Chess Pieces

Peacock Feathers

Horses

Pomegranates

Peacocks

Squirrels

My Gratitude

Making a living as an artist is a daring way to live, and it takes tremendous dedication to bring any art to life and share it with the world. Thank you for supporting the arts, and honoring my efforts buying this book.

Many thanks to the Girl Genius group for their inspiration, encouragement and friendship that helped me bring this project to life, and to Sanae for her many years of friendship and for her excellent creative direction and digital skills. Thank you also to my studio friends: Jacqueline for the initial idea to produce a coloring book for adults and Sonserae for generously sharing her equipment. It would be impossible to name all of you but I want to express gratitude to my many friends who have offered their support, shared their insights, and urged me onward. Finally, thank you to my husband Boyce who is so much more that an editor, confidant, friend and lover. I couldn't imagine doing this project without his support.

About reproduction of this book

.

Visual Index

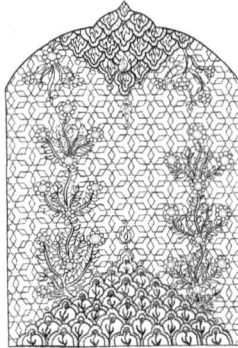   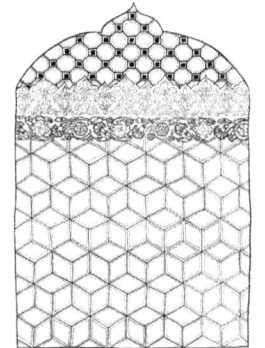

   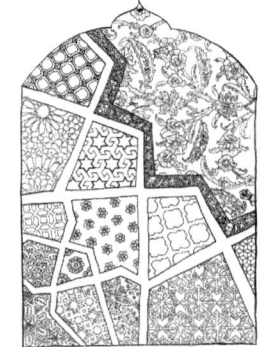